SOUTH AMERICA
TODAY

ARGENTINA

SOUTH AMERICA
TODAY

ARGENTINA

Charles J. Shields

Mason Crest Publishers
Philadelphia

Produced by OTTN Publishing, Stockton, N.J.

Mason Crest Publishers
370 Reed Road
Broomall, PA 19008
www.masoncrest.com

Printed and bound in the Hashemite Kingdom of Jordan.

CPSIA Compliance Information: Batch #03262010-SAT. For further information, contact Mason Crest Publishers at 1-866-MCP-Book.

3 5 7 9 8 6 4 2

Library of Congress Cataloging-in-Publication Data

Shields, Charles J., 1951-
Argentina / Charles J. Shields.
p. cm. — (South America today)
Includes index.
ISBN 978-1-4222-0631-7 (hardcover) — ISBN 978-1-4222-0698-0 (pbk.)
1. Argentina—Juvenile literature. [1. Argentina.] I. Title.
F2808.2.S55 2008
982—dc22

2008032253

SOUTH AMERICA TODAY

Argentina
Bolivia
Brazil
Chile
Colombia
South America: Facts & Figures
Ecuador
Guyana
Paraguay
Peru
Suriname
Uruguay
Venezuela

Table of Contents

Discovering South America

James D. Henderson

South America is a cornucopia of natural resources, a treasure house of ecological variety. It is also a continent of striking human diversity and geographic extremes. Yet in spite of that, most South Americans share a set of cultural similarities. Most of the continent's inhabitants are properly termed "Latin" Americans. This means that they speak a Romance language (one closely related to Latin), particularly Spanish or Portuguese. It means, too, that most practice Roman Catholicism and share the Mediterranean cultural patterns brought by the Spanish and Portuguese who settled the continent over five centuries ago.

Still, it is never hard to spot departures from these cultural norms. Bolivia, Peru, and Ecuador, for example, have significant Indian populations who speak their own languages and follow their own customs. In Paraguay the main Indian language, Guaraní, is accepted as official along with Spanish. Nor are all South Americans Catholics. Today Protestantism is making steady gains, while in Brazil many citizens practice African religions right along with Catholicism and Protestantism.

South America is a lightly populated continent, having just 6 percent of the world's people. It is also the world's most tropical continent, for a larger percentage of its land falls between the tropics of Cancer and Capricorn than is the case with any other continent. The world's driest desert is there, the Atacama in northern Chile, where no one has ever seen a drop of rain fall. And the world's wettest place is there too, the Chocó region of Colombia, along that country's border with Panama. There it rains almost every day. South America also has some of the world's highest mountains, the Andes,

Buenos Aires at dusk, facing north along the Avenida 9 de Julio.

and its greatest river, the Amazon.

So welcome to South America! Through this colorfully illustrated series of books you will travel through 12 countries, from giant Brazil to small Suriname. On your way you will learn about the geography, the history, the economy, and the people of each one. Geared to the needs of teachers and students, each volume contains book and web sources for further study, a chronology, project and report ideas, and even recipes of tasty and easy-to-prepare dishes popular in the countries studied. Each volume describes the country's national holidays and the cities and towns where they are held. And each book is indexed.

You are embarking on a voyage of discovery that will take you to lands not so far away, but as interesting and exotic as any in the world.

Argentina is a large, geographically diverse land, as these two photos suggest. *Opposite:* A river cuts through the rain forest in the Paraná Plateau region of northeastern Argentina. *Right:* The massive Perito Moreno Glacier in Los Glaciares National Park, on the southwestern edge of Patagonia.

1 Land of Contrasts

ARGENTINA, THE WORLD'S eighth-largest country, makes up almost the entire southern half of South America—an area known as the Southern Cone. It is a land of great natural beauty and great contrasts. Some of the world's tallest mountains can be found in Argentina. So, too, can enormous grassland plains and a windswept plateau that seems to stretch on forever. Along with mighty waterfalls and numerous alpine lakes, Argentina is home to wide deserts and steamy swamps.

Six Distinct Regions

The second-largest South American country after Brazil, Argentina borders Chile to the west (separated by the Andes Mountains), Bolivia and Paraguay to the north (separated by rivers), and Brazil and Uruguay to the northeast (also separated by rivers). Its long coastline, about 3,100 miles (4,989 kilometers) in length, faces the Atlantic Ocean. Triangular in shape, Argentina stretches approximately 2,300 miles (3,701 km) from its broad northern region near the tropic of Capricorn to Tierra del Fuego, an island shared with Chile, in the south.

Argentina can be divided into six geographical regions—the Paraná Plateau, the Gran Chaco, the Pampas, the Monte, the plateau known as Patagonia, and the Andes Mountains.

The Paraná Plateau in the extreme northeast is an extension of the highlands of southern Brazil. It is the wettest part of Argentina and, despite its dense forest cover, is extremely hot during the summer. Tobacco, timber, and yerba maté (a tea-like beverage) are the chief products here. The spectacular Iguazú Falls (spelled Iguaçu in Portuguese-speaking Brazil) are in a national park located at the point where Argentina, Brazil, and Paraguay meet.

In northern Argentina, the Gran Chaco is a region Argentina shares with Bolivia, Paraguay, and Brazil. Mainly a flat *alluvial* plain with a subtropical climate, the Gran Chaco stays flooded at certain times of the year. Marshlands remain for long periods because of poor drainage. Livestock, cotton, and wood from the quebracho tree are the region's main products.

South of the Gran Chaco is the Pampas, a vast, monotonous natural grassland 400 miles (644 km) wide from the Atlantic Ocean to the Andean foothills. The deep, rich soil of the Pampas, which is composed largely of a fine sand, clay, and silt almost wholly free of pebbles and rocks, is ideal for growing grain and provides most of the wealth of the country. From this region come most of Argentina's agricultural exports: wheat, alfalfa, corn, and *flax.* The Pampas is also home to cattle and sheep ranching. Dairy farms appear near Buenos Aires. This section of Argentina has the most extensive network of roads and railroads in South America.

The Monte is an arid region in the shadow of the Andes. Its vegetation varies from short grasses in the east to cacti in the west. Scattered throughout the great desert stretches are small but highly productive oases such as Jujuy, Salta, San Miguel de Tucumán, San Juan, and Mendoza. These large towns were settled from Peru and Upper Peru (Bolivia) in the second half of the 16th century. In the 19th century, railroads linked them to the east coast, carrying their wine, sugar, fruit, corn, and livestock. The mines of the Monte yield lead, zinc, tin, copper, and salt. Oil is drawn from the ground here, too.

Occupying the southern part of Argentina is Patagonia, a gigantic, bleak, and windswept plateau. Several large rivers flow in deep valleys eastward across Patagonia to the sea. Its cool grazing grounds support enormous flocks of sheep. Patagonia also holds significant reserves of oil and coal. But

A herd of goats and cows grazes near the village of Purmamarca, in the dry, rugged Monte region.

Iguazú Falls, located at the point where Argentina, Brazil, and Paraguay meet, is breathtakingly beautiful. The falls (there are about 275 different cataracts)

the poor soils of Patagonia and its cool and dry climate do not favor agriculture without irrigation. Patagonia is sparsely populated and largely undeveloped, with a few small river-mouth ports on the Atlantic coast such as Viedma, Rawson, Puerto Deseado, and Río Gallegos. Ushuaia, in the Tierra del Fuego region, is the southernmost town in the world.

stretch for more than 2 miles (3.2 km), and some 176,570 cubic feet of water passes over the edge every second, dropping more than 260 feet (80 meters).

Soaring Mountains, Deep Rivers, and Lakes

The western part of Argentina lies within the Andes, the great mountain system of the South American continent. For long stretches, the *continental divide* marks the Argentine-Chilean *frontier*. The mountains of the

Quick Facts: The Geography of Argentina

Location: southern South America, bordering the Atlantic Ocean, between Chile and Uruguay

Area: (slightly less than three-tenths the size of the United States)
total: 1,068,296 square miles (2,766,890 sq km)
land: 1,056,636 square miles (2,736,690 sq km)
water: 11,660 square miles (30,200 sq km)

Borders: Bolivia, 517 miles (832 km); Brazil, 760 miles (1,224 km); Chile, 3,200 miles (5,150 km); Paraguay, 1,168 miles (1,880 km); Uruguay, 360 miles (579 km)

Climate: mostly temperate; arid in southeast; subantarctic in southwest

Terrain: rich plains of the Pampas in northern half, flat to rolling plateau of Patagonia in south, rugged Andes Mountains along western border

Elevation extremes:
lowest point: Salinas Chicas (located on Valdés Peninsula)—131 feet (40 meters) below sea level
highest point: Cerro Aconcagua—22,834 feet (6,960 meters)

Natural hazards: San Miguel de Tucumán and Mendoza areas in the Andes subject to earthquakes; pamperos are violent windstorms that can strike the Pampas and northeast; heavy flooding

Source: Adapted from CIA World Factbook 2001

Patagonian Andes, which form a natural boundary between Argentina and Chile, are comparatively low, seldom exceeding about 12,000 feet (3,660 meters) in elevation. But from the northern end of this range to the Bolivian frontier, the main Andean *cordillera* begins. The peaks here rise above 21,000 feet (6,405 meters) in some places. Aconcagua at 22,834 feet (6,960 meters) is the highest peak in the Western Hemisphere, and the tallest mountain in the world outside central Asia. Several parallel ranges and spurs of the Andes project deeply into northwestern Argentina.

The chief rivers of Argentina are the Paraná, which runs through the north-central portion of the country; the Paraguay, the main tributary of the Paraná; and the Río de la Plata, the great *estuary* at the confluence of the Paraná and Uruguay Rivers. The Uruguay forms part of the boundary with Uruguay. The Paraná-Uruguay system is navigable by ship and boat for about 2,000 miles (3,219 km). A famed scenic attraction, Iguazú Falls, is located on a tributary of the Paraná. Other important rivers of Argentina are the Río Colorado, the Río Salado, and the Río Negro. The water system of Argentina includes numerous lakes, particularly among the foothills of the Patagonian Andes. The best known are in the alpine lake country around the resort town of San Carlos de Bariloche.

From Subtropical to Cold

Argentina's climate varies from subtropical in the north to cold and windswept in the south. Temperate and dry areas are found throughout much of the country. The weather in the Andes region is extreme—irregular rainfall, flash floods in summer, searing heat, snow at higher elevations, and the *zonda*—a hot, dry wind. Rains in the lowlands create swampy forests and upland *savanna*, but rainfall decreases from east to west. Shallow summer flooding is common in the east. Patagonia is mild year-round in the east and glacial in the south.

Because Argentina is located in the Southern Hemisphere, its seasons are opposite those of the United States. In Buenos Aires the average temperature range is 67°F to 86°F (20°C to 30°C) in January, and 46°F to 60°F (8°C to 16°C) in July. In Mendoza, in the foothills of the Andes to the west, the average tem-

The wide range of climatological conditions in Argentina produces a great variety of vegetation, from desert cacti to the tropical heliconia pictured here.

perature range is 60°F to 90°F (16°C to 32°C) in January and 35°F to 59°F (2°C to 15°C) in July. Much higher temperatures prevail near the tropic of Capricorn in the north, where extremes as high as 113°F (45°C) are sometimes reached. The weather is generally cold in the higher Andes, Patagonia, and Tierra del Fuego. In the western section of Patagonia winter temperatures average about 32°F (0°C). Along the Atlantic coast, the warmth of the water makes the air warmer than inland.

Precipitation in Argentina varies by region. More than 60 inches (152 centimeters) falls annually in the extreme north, but conditions gradually become semiarid to the south and west. Near Buenos Aires annual rainfall is about 37 inches (94 cm). In the vicinity of Mendoza annual rainfall is about 7 inches (18 cm).

Plants and Animals

The warm and moist northeastern area of Argentina supports tropical plants, including such trees as palm, rosewood, lignum vitae, jacaranda, and red quebracho. The deserts of northwestern Argentina feature cacti and other thorny plants.

Grasses cover most of the Pampas. Trees are not widespread there or in Patagonia, except for drought-resistant types such as the eucalyptus, sycamore, and acacia. The chief types of vegetation in Patagonia are herbs, shrubs, grasses, and brambles. On the other hand, the cool and breezy Andean foothills of Patagonia and parts of Tierra del Fuego support flourishing growths of conifers, especially fir, cypress, pine, and cedar.

Animals are most abundant in the north. The mammals in these regions include several species of monkeys, jaguars, pumas, ocelots, anteaters, tapirs, peccaries, and raccoons. Native birds include the flamingo and various hummingbirds and parrots. In the Pampas are armadillos, foxes, martens, wildcats, hare, deer, ostrich-like birds called rheas, hawks, falcons, herons, plovers, and partridges. Some of these animals are also found in Patagonia. The cold Andean regions are the habitat of llamas, guanacos (a lowland relative of the upper-Andean llama), vicuñas, alpacas, and condors. Fish abound in coastal waters, lakes, and streams.

Argentina has created more than 20 national parks or preserves that protect rare wildlife such as the caiman (or *yacaré*), puma, guanaco, rhea, Andean condor, flamingo, various marine mammals, and unusual seabirds such as Magellanic penguins. Thorn forests, virgin rain forests, flowering cacti, and extensive forests of monkey-puzzle trees and southern beech are also protected.

The wing of an eagle statue frames the National Congress Building (*opposite*). Traders on the floor of the stock exchange in Buenos Aires (*right*). Since its establishment as a federal republic in the 19th century, Argentina has experienced many difficulties on the path to democracy, economic prosperity, and social stability.

2 The Quest for Stability

AFTER INDEPENDENCE FROM Spain, Argentina successfully steered a course toward becoming one of the most prosperous and influential countries in the hemisphere. Following World War II, however, tensions between pro- and anti-democratic forces—complete with periods of repressive military rule—severely disrupted Argentine society. Economic crises also threatened the nation's stability. Through the first years of the 21st century, Argentina struggled to regain its footing.

From Prehistory to Colonization

Little is known about the earliest inhabitants of Argentina. Some of these people were members of *nomadic* tribes, while others engaged in agriculture. The people in the south primarily hunted and fished. In the northwest, near

Bolivia and the Andes, lived a people known as the Diaguita. The Diaguita built a permanent civilization around farming. They also successfully prevented the powerful Inca people from invading their lands.

Perhaps because the Diaguita had a history of resisting incursions, the first Spaniard to land in Argentina, Juan de Solís, was killed in 1516. But the search for a southwest passage to Asia and the East Indies soon brought other explorers, including Ferdinand Magellan in 1520, and Sebastian Cabot in 1526. Cabot sailed up the Paraná and Paraguay Rivers. His delight in finding beautiful ornaments made by the local people may be responsible for the names Río de la Plata (meaning "Silver River") and Argentina (meaning "of silver").

In 1536 Pedro de Mendoza, a Spanish soldier appointed military governor of the area between the Río de la Plata and the Strait of Magellan, founded the colony of Buenos Aires. Resistance from the *indigenous* people of the area forced the Spanish to abandon Buenos Aires five years later, however. As happened throughout Latin America, though, disease would eventually decimate the native inhabitants and pave the way for Spanish conquest. Native peoples had no immunity to such deadly diseases as smallpox, which had existed in Europe for centuries but which was unknown in the Western Hemisphere before the arrival of Columbus. By 1553 the Spanish had established their first permanent settlement in present-day Argentina, Santiago del Estero. Gradually they extended their control southward toward the Río de la Plata, founding Santa Fe in 1573 and a new settlement at Buenos Aires in 1580.

In 1620, the Spanish viceroyalty of Peru (originally set up to administer the lands of the former Inca Empire) assumed administrative control of the Río de la Plata region. But poor commercial policies hampered colonization

Three hunters of the Ona tribe pose for a photograph, circa 1895. The nomadic Ona had roamed Tierra del Fuego for some 9,000 years, but early white settlers slaughtered them, and the last full-blooded Ona is believed to have died in 1999. Unlike many other Latin American nations, Argentina has seen comparatively little intermarriage between whites and Amerindians.

of the area for 100 years. Nevertheless, Buenos Aires grew steadily, thanks in large measure to its bustling trade in smuggled goods. By the mid-1700s, its population approached 20,000. In 1776 the huge territory occupied by present-day Argentina, Bolivia, Paraguay, and Uruguay was separated from Peru and incorporated as the Viceroyalty of the Río de la Plata.

Independence

In 1808 Napoleon Bonaparte, the emperor of France, deposed Spain's king, Ferdinand VII, and installed his brother on the Spanish throne. Across the Atlantic Ocean in Buenos Aires, the Spanish colonists refused to recognize Joseph Bonaparte as Spain's king. They ousted the colony's government on May 25, 1810, and set up a provisional government loyal to Ferdinand. Eventually, though, many colonists in the Río de la Plata region—like colonists throughout the Spanish possessions in Central and South America—came to favor complete independence.

José de San Martín, born in an Uruguay River town in what is now Argentina, emerged as a brilliant general for the pro-independence forces. He raised a formidable army on Argentine soil, crossed the Andes, and liberated Chile. Later he marched into Lima and declared the independence of Peru.

Meanwhile, in 1816, representatives from the various provinces in what is today Argentina met in San Miguel de Tucumán. On July 9, they proclaimed their complete independence from Spain and announced the formation of the United Provinces of South America. Unfortunately, they never agreed on what form the new government should take. A brief civil war broke out in 1819, and a decade of chaos followed.

Finally, in 1829, the political turmoil began to be resolved with the election of General Juan Manuel de Rosas as governor of Buenos Aires Province. Rosas skillfully extended his influence over the other provinces, and the United Provinces became the Argentine Confederation, under his control.

Birth of the Argentine Republic

Stability came with a price, however. Rosas ruled with an iron hand, crushing all opposition to his authority. The dictator was finally ousted in 1852 by a revolutionary group led by General Justo José Urquiza, a former governor of Entre Ríos Province.

In 1853 a federal constitution was adopted, and Urquiza became the first president of the Argentine Republic. The following year, however, Buenos Aires Province proclaimed its independence. After a brief war in 1859, Buenos Aires was defeated and brought back into the republic, but another revolt flared in 1861. This time, forces from Buenos Aires Province, under the command of General Bartolomé Mitre, emerged victorious.

In 1862 a national convention elected Mitre to the presidency and designated the city of Buenos Aires as the national capital. Buenos Aires Province, the wealthiest and most populous in the nation, had risen to a position of dominance.

Successes and Setbacks

Following the settling of a series of border disputes with neighboring countries, Argentina made remarkable economic and social progress in the 50 years after 1880. During the first decade of the 20th century, the country emerged as the leading nation of South America. In 1914, Argentina helped mediate a serious dispute between the United States and Mexico. Argentina remained neutral during World War I (1914–18) but played a major role as supplier of foodstuffs to the Allies.

The long period of growth ended with the world economic crisis that began in 1929. Joblessness and other hardships created deep social and political unrest. The year before the presidential elections of 1937, *Fascist* organizations became increasingly active. The Argentine right-wing parties united in the so-called National Front, which openly called for a dictatorship to protect property. The National Front successfully elected Roberto M. Ortiz to the presidency, but Ortiz stunned his supporters by taking vigorous steps to strengthen democracy in Argentina.

In 1943, however, a group of military officers seized control of the government. General Pedro Ramírez, one of the leaders of the group, assumed the presidency. He outlawed political parties, muzzled the press, and rolled

With significant help from Eva Duarte, his beautiful and popular wife, Juan Domingo Perón dominated Argentine politics in the mid-20th century. His regime was marked by uneven economic progress and the suppression of civil liberties.

back the democratic progress made under Ortiz and his successor.

Just a year later, another military *junta* ousted Ramírez. Its most powerful member was an army colonel named Juan Domingo Perón.

The Perón Years

Perón won the presidential elections held in 1946 and soon set about consolidating his power by intimidating and arresting opponents in the press, the legislature, and the judiciary. He was reelected by a wide margin in 1951, though by then he had become a dictator in all but name. His Peronist Party would dominate Argentine politics for many years.

Perón's second wife, Eva Duarte de Perón—called Evita by the Argentine people—reinforced his political strength. She was especially popular with the working classes, from which her husband drew his most fervent support. Although she never held an official government post, Evita acted informally as minister of health and labor, establishing a national charitable organization and awarding generous wage increases to labor unions.

Workers responded by pledging political support for Perón.

Eventually, though, the armed forces tired of Perón's strong-arm tactics and removed him in a *coup*. Perón went into exile in 1955, three years after Evita's death. Argentina entered a long period of military dictatorships with brief intervals of constitutional government.

Perón returned to power in 1973. His third wife, Isabel Martínez de Perón, was elected vice president. After her husband's death in 1974, she became the Western Hemisphere's first female chief of state, assuming control of a nation teetering on the brink of economic and political collapse.

In 1975, terrorist acts by left- and right-wing groups killed some 700 people. The cost of living rose 355 percent. Strikes and demonstrations were constant. On March 24, 1976, a military junta led by army commander Lieutenant General Jorge Rafael Videla seized power and imposed martial law.

Wars Domestic and Foreign

The military began the so-called Dirty War, which was waged not against a foreign country but against Argentina's own citizens. Its goal was to restore order—and to eliminate opponents of the regime. According to the Argentine Commission for Human Rights, more than 10,000 political arrests were made during the Dirty War; in addition, the junta and its allies committed some 2,300 political murders and were responsible for the disappearances of 20,000 to 30,000 Argentine citizens—most of whom were probably also murdered.

Although the junta's brutal tactics suppressed political opposition, the economy remained in chaos. In March 1981 Videla was deposed by Field Marshal Roberto Viola, who in turn was succeeded by Lieutenant General

Leopoldo Galtieri.

Galtieri, hoping perhaps to deflect attention from the country's domestic problems, ordered the invasion of the British-held Falkland Islands on April 2, 1982. Argentina had long claimed the sparsely populated Falklands, which Argentines call Las Islas Malvinas. Galtieri's gamble proved disastrous. Great Britain sent troops to the Falklands and decisively defeated the Argentines. Galtieri resigned in disgrace three days after Argentina's surrender.

Major General Reynaldo Bignone took over the presidency on June 14. Demonstrations calling for greater democracy competed with marches to protest *inflation*, which was exceeding 900 percent.

In the presidential election of October 1983, Raúl Alfonsín, leader of the Radical Civic Union, handed the Peronist Party its first defeat since strongman Juan Perón had founded the party more than three decades earlier. However, growing unemployment and quadruple-digit inflation led to a Peronist victory in the elections of May 1989. Alfonsín resigned a month later

Inaugurated as president on December 10, 2007, Cristina Fernández inherited a fragile but recovering economy. A Peronist former senator, Fernández has alienated many citizens with tough legislation, such as higher taxes on agricultural products.

in the wake of riots over high food prices, in favor of the new Peronist president, Carlos Menem. In 1991, Menem promoted economic reforms designed to reverse decades of state intervention and *protectionism*. Menem had the constitution changed in 1994 to allow him to serve for a second term.

Throughout the 1990s, Argentina won international praise for continued reforms and for its conclusion of a new arrangement with the International Monetary Fund at the end of 1997. Beginning in September 1998, however, Argentina faced its worst recession in a decade, and unemployment hit 15 percent in August 1999.

Collapse and Recovery

In December 1999 Fernando de la Rua became president. Despite economic austerity plans and over $20 billion in international emergency aid, the recession continued. In December 2001, as Argentina neared economic collapse and riots ensued, de la Rua resigned.

On January 1, 2002, Eduardo Duhalde became Argentina's fifth president in two weeks. Argentina then defaulted on its $155 billion foreign debt. The government's devaluation of the Argentine peso upended the banking industry and wiped out middle-class savings. Nearly 300,000 people left the country.

In 2003, Peronist Néstor Kirchner was elected president. He improved relations with other Latin American nations and restructured foreign debt. The economy recovered considerably, but the authority Kirchner gave himself caused some worry. Kirchner's wife, Cristina Fernández, became the next president in 2007. She pledged to continue economic growth and stabilize social tension.

Unemployed workers demonstrate in Buenos Aires, January 2002 (*opposite*). The government's decision that month to allow Argentina's currency (*right*) to float freely plunged the banking industry into crisis, wiped out much of the savings of the middle class, and helped push joblessness to 25 percent by midyear.

3 An Underachieving Economy

ARGENTINA IS ONE of the world's leading cattle- and grain-producing nations. It produces enough agricultural products not only to fill its own market needs, but also to export surpluses to foreign markets. In recent decades, manufacturing and mining industries have shown marked growth, too. The country's main manufacturing enterprises are meatpacking and flour-milling plants.

But economic growth in 2000 was a disappointing 0.8 percent because of the government's inability to pay down its national debt. In the first years of the 21st century, foreign investors believed Argentina's economy was too risky. Problems with bank failures, joblessness, and inflation continued to slow the nation's economic recovery.

Argentina is rich in resources and has a well-educated workforce. It is a major producer of agricultural goods, cattle, and oil. Argentina is one of the world's largest exporters of soybeans, wheat, and meat, even though agriculture accounts for only about 10 percent of its output.

The services sector—banking and tourism mainly—accounts for over half of Argentina's *gross domestic product (GDP)*. According to statistics compiled by the CIA, Argentina's GDP in 2007 stood at $523.7 billion, making it the world's 25th largest economy. Manufacturing forms the largest part of the industrial sector, which accounts for 35 percent of the GDP and nearly one-fourth of the employment. But Argentina's industry, while ahead of many of its neighbors, lags behind other highly industrialized nations. In fact, despite abundant natural resources and a very capable workforce, the Argentine economy has a long record of instability.

Slow Slide into Crisis

Before World War II, Argentina's economy was among the world's strongest. From the 1940s until the early 1990s, however, the nation experienced slow growth and high inflation. The inflation rate peaked in 1989 at more than 3,000 percent. In 1990, following the near collapse of the country's financial system, the government enacted a program of economic austerity. It put into private hands numerous state-run companies such as railroads and utilities. Profits from the sale of the state-run companies were used to pay down the national debt. Hundreds of thousands of workers lost their jobs.

In 1991, Argentina enacted radical reforms in its financial system, the most important of which was to peg the worth of the peso to the U.S. dollar.

Cattle graze on the Pampas, the vast, fertile grassland that supports Argentina's world-famous cattle industry as well as large-scale grain farming. Argentina ranks among the world's leading exporters of wheat, corn, and oats.

At first, the economy rebounded, spurred by major investment from abroad. Inflation fell sharply. But instability in the international financial markets—specifically the collapse of the Mexican peso in 1995 and upheavals in Russia three years later—took a toll on Argentina's fragile economy. Conditions worsened in 1999 as Argentina's GDP fell by 3 percent.

The government's earlier decision to peg the peso to the U.S. dollar came under fire. Critics claimed that it added to Argentina's economic problems by causing the peso to be overvalued. In January 2002 the government ended the practice of linking the value of the peso to the U.S. dollar. By mid-January 2002 the Argentine peso was trading for 71 U.S. cents. By June the peso had lost about 70 percent of its value, fueling another round of high inflation.

Public unrest fueled protests, some of which turned violent when it was announced that the value of savings accounts had dropped by 50 percent or more. The government ordered all savings accounts temporarily frozen, and many Argentines found themselves unable to buy basic necessities. When financial activity began again, federal and other major employers could only pay their workers in government bonds. Public anger and frustration led to constant, nationwide protests.

The crisis of 2002 abated slowly thanks to aggressive government programs and international debt restructuring. Argentina's economy grew at least 8% per year from 2003 onward—recovering enough to drastically reduce debt, curb inflation, and entice some who emigrated to return. However, many Argentineans suspect the government tampers with statistics to hide bad news. For example, inflation was officially estimated at 8.8% in 2007, but economists said the rate might have been twice as high.

Buenos Aires, one of the largest cities in South America, is Argentina's chief commercial, industrial, and financial center. It also serves as the transportation hub of southern South America.

Quick Facts: The Economy of Argentina

Gross domestic product (GDP*): $523.7 billion (purchasing power parity)

GDP per capita: $13,300

Inflation: 8.8% (official rate; disputed)

Natural resources: fertile plains of the Pampas, lead, zinc, tin, copper, iron ore, manganese, petroleum, uranium

Agriculture (9.5% of GDP): sunflower seeds, lemons, soybeans, grapes, corn, tobacco, peanuts, tea, wheat, livestock

Services (56.5% of GDP): banking, tourism

Industry (34% of GDP): food processing, motor vehicles, consumer durables, textiles, chemicals and petrochemicals, printing, metallurgy, steel

Foreign trade (2000 est.):
Exports—$54.6 billion: soybeans and derivatives, petroleum and gas, vehicles, corn, wheat
Imports—$42.6 billion: machinery, motor vehicles, petroleum and natural gas, organic chemicals, plastics

Currency exchange rate: 3.026 Argentine pesos = U.S. $1 (August 2008)

*GDP is the total value of goods and services produced in one year.

Figures are 2007 estimates unless otherwise noted.
Sources: CIA World Factbook 2008, Bloomberg.com.

Economic Strengths

Per capita income in Argentina has historically been among the highest in South America. And, in contrast to many Latin American countries, the wealth is not concentrated in the hands of a very few; Argentina has a relatively large middle class. Still, because of the country's continuing economic problems, an estimated 23 percent of Argentina's citizens were living below the poverty line in 2007.

Although Argentina's economy has traditionally been based on agriculture, the industrial and service sectors have grown in importance in recent years. Argentine industry, developed after World War I, enabled the country to supply nearly all the major needs of its consumers. Today, the chief manufacturing industry is food processing—in particular meatpacking, flour milling, and canning. Textiles, leather goods, and chemicals are also major products. Argentina's main imports are metals, machinery, and other manufactured goods.

Most of the principal cities of Argentina and most of its industry are found in the Pampas. Buenos Aires, a port city on the Río de la Plata, is one of the largest cities in South America. It is also the chief industrial center and transportation hub of southern South America. Surrounding it are smaller industrial cities.

Elsewhere on the Pampas are La Plata, a meatpacking and oil-refining center; Rosario, the third-largest city of Argentina, an iron, steel, and oil-refining center, and a huge grain port on the Paraná River; Santa Fe, a northern commercial and industrial center at the junction of the Salado and Paraná Rivers; Mar del Plata, a resort and fishing center on the Atlantic Ocean; and Bahía Blanca, the largest Argentine port directly on the Atlantic Ocean. On the western edge of the Pampas is Córdoba, the nation's second-largest city.

The Pampas is Argentina's chief agricultural area. However, since the 1930s there has been a great rise in production in other areas, especially in the oases of the Monte and the irrigated valleys of northern Patagonia. Livestock (cattle and sheep) and grains have long been the foundation of Argentina's wealth. Its cattle herds are among the world's finest. Argentina also ranks with the United States, Canada, and Australia as one of the world's largest exporters of wheat, corn, flax, oats, beef, mutton, hides, and wool. Its other

A coal-mining operation in southern Patagonia, which has large deposits of low-grade coal.

agricultural products include oilseeds, sorghum, soybeans, and sugar beets. Argentina is the world's largest source of tannin and linseed oil.

Although Argentina has a variety of minerals, they don't exist in large enough supply to completely support the country's industries. Local oil and gas production has made the nation self-sufficient in energy. Pipelines connect the oil and gas fields with Buenos Aires and other major refining centers. Southern Patagonia has large deposits of low-grade coal.

Argentina has vast economic potential. Yet high unemployment and a massive national debt remain as major obstacles to the fulfillment of that potential.

Argentina's rich culture has been influenced by the peoples of many European nations, not just Spain. *Opposite*: Drummers in traditional dress at a parade in Buenos Aires. *Right*: A modern-day gaucho, descendant of the legendary cowboys of the Pampas.

4 A Rich Mosaic: The People and Culture

ARGENTINA IS A nation with a rich Spanish heritage, strongly influenced since the 19th century by European immigration. Today, over 90 percent of the population is of European ancestry. Unlike most Latin American countries, Argentina has relatively few mestizos (persons of mixed European and Native American ancestry), although their number has increased in recent times. A lively interest is maintained in the nation's history, especially as symbolized by the gaucho (cowboy)—the solitary, independent ranch-hand on the Pampas. In the arts, Argentines have frequently looked to France for their models in literature, music, and painting. Argentina gave the Western world its own highly stylized dance, the tango.

Fanatical about *el fútbol*: an Argentine soccer fan shows his colors.

A Flood of Immigrants

Between 1850 and 1940, some 6,608,700 Europeans settled in Argentina. Italian, Spanish (including Basque), French, German, British, Swiss, and eastern European immigrants came to Argentina during the 1880s. Other large influxes of Europeans occurred in the 1930s and following World War II. The European immigrant groups each took different roles in Argentine society. Basque and Irish immigrants gravitated toward sheep raising, Germans and Italians established farms, and British invested in developing the country's banking and transportation systems.

The Argentine cowboy, or gaucho—a nomadic herder of the Pampas—is a legendary national symbol. Many gauchos were people of mixed Spanish and black descent who had crossed the border from Brazil to escape slavery. Gaucho life, vividly depicted in José Hernández's 1872 folk epic *Martín Fierro*, still holds a firm grip on the Argentine imagination—even though Argentina by the 1990s had a mainly urban population, with more than four-fifths of its people living in cities and towns. More than a third of the total population lives in and around Buenos Aires.

The mestizo portion of Argentina's population is small, except in the northwest; unlike other Latin American countries, Argentina has seen little mixing between European and indigenous peoples. The native population and its culture steadily declined after the coming of the Europeans and remains strong only in parts of the Gran Chaco and the Andean highlands. Today mestizo and indigenous peoples make up less than 5 percent of Argentina's population.

Churches and Schools

Ninety percent of Argentina's population is Roman Catholic. By law, the president and vice president must be Roman Catholic. But native beliefs and customs have created a special brand of Argentine Roman Catholicism. Spiritualism (a belief that spirits of the dead communicate with the living) and honoring the dead are widespread customs. Pilgrimages to cemeteries to pay respects to deceased relatives and famous people are common.

In addition to Roman Catholicism, Judaism, Protestantism, and a number of other Christian and non-Christian religions are practiced. The Jewish community, while accounting for only about 2 percent of Argentina's people, is the largest in Latin America and the fifth largest in the world.

Spanish is the country's official language, although many Argentines understand Italian as well. English-speakers pronounce words like the British. There are 17 native languages, including Quechua, Mapuche, Guaraní, Tobas, and Matacos.

Education is free and *compulsory* from ages 5 to 14. The official attendance rate is 94 percent. Argentina's *literacy* rate of 97 percent is one of the highest in Latin America. Argentina has 25 national universities and many private universities. The principal institution is the University of Buenos Aires, founded in 1821.

European Influences

European influences can be seen all through Argentina's art, architecture, literature, and lifestyle. Many Argentines are educated in Europe. Several famous Argentine writers lived and wrote in Europe for at least part of their careers. And Argentina has produced some of the most acclaimed writers of the past 50 years, including Jorge Luis Borges, Julio Cortázar, Ernesto Sábato, Manuel Puig, and Osvaldo Soriano.

Buenos Aires in particular resembles a European city in art, music, and architecture. The leading library of Argentina is the National Library (1810) in Buenos Aires, which has about 1.9 million volumes. Prominent among the many museums in Buenos Aires are the Argentine Museum of Natural Sciences, the National Museum of Fine Arts, and such private collections as the International Art Gallery. The Museum of La Plata is famous for its collections of reptile fossils. The National Symphony Orchestra is based in Buenos Aires, and the opera company of the city is housed in the Teatro Colón, built in 1908.

Much Argentine painting in the 19th century portrayed gaucho themes. Scenes of town life also figured prominently.

The most important elements of traditional Argentine music are the gaucho folk song and folk dance. Music that reflects Native American, European, North American, and African influences can be heard live or on the radio, too.

The tango, which originated among the lower classes in Buenos Aires around the 1880s and went on to become a favorite in ballrooms throughout much of the world, is Argentina's most famous contribution to modern music and dance. Astor Piazzolla, a highly productive 20th-century tango composer, bandleader, and performer, incorporated jazz and classical influences in his works. During the 1920s and 1930s Argentine tango singer Carlos Gardel was idolized throughout Latin America.

When it comes to dining, beef is found everywhere. Mixed grills (*parrilladas*) are popular, serving up a cut of just about every part of the animal. In Buenos Aires, restaurant dining doesn't usually begin until 9:00 P.M. Main courses usually consist of an *asado*, or barbecued beef dish. *Bife de chorizo* (sirloin steak) or *empanadas* (meat pies) are favorites, too. The national deserts are *dulce de leche*, a milk jelly; and *alfajores*, Argentine sweets made from *dulce de leche*.

"Coming Out" Parties

In Argentina, as in other Spanish-speaking countries of Latin America, a girl's 15th birthday, or "*quince años*," is an important occasion. The girl's family typically throws an all-night dinner-dance party to celebrate.

The tango, which developed among lower-class immigrants in Buenos Aires, ranks as Argentina's most significant contribution to modern dance and music.

A street musician strums his guitar in the fashionable Recoleta district of Buenos Aires. Traditional gaucho music remains quite popular in Argentina, even among the nation's city-dwellers.

If the family is Catholic, family members and guests attend Mass in the morning before the party begins. At the end of the Mass the priest offers a blessing for the *quinceañera*, as the girl is called. For the occasion, she will usually be wearing a long dress, like a bride's. Afterward the *quinceañera* receives the guests, who give her presents.

The party includes dinner in a banquet room. As the time for the toasts arrives, the presents are opened and a huge birthday cake, filled with surprises, is cut. Friends take hold of one of the ribbons coming from the cake and pull. On the other end is their surprise. One of these is usually a ring, meaning marriage.

After the cutting of the cake, the traditional waltz begins. The girl's father

Quick Facts: The People of Argentina

Population: 40,677,348

Ethnic groups: white (mostly Spanish and Italian) 97%, mestizo (mixed white and Amerindian ancestry), Amerindian, or other non-white groups 3%

Age structure:
0–14 years: 24.6%
15–64 years: 64.6%
65 years and over: 10.8%

Population growth rate: 0.917%

Birth rate: 16.32 births/1,000 population

Death rate: 7.54 deaths/1,000 population

Infant mortality rate: 13.87 deaths/1,000 live births

Life expectancy at birth:
total population: 76.52 years
male: 72.81 years
female: 80.43 years

Total fertility rate: 2.09 children born/woman

Religions: nominally Roman Catholic 92%, Protestant 2%, Jewish 2%, other 4%

Languages: Spanish (official), English, Italian, German, French

Literacy rate (percentage of people age 15 and over who can read and write): 97.2% (2006 est.)

Figures are 2008 estimates unless otherwise noted.

Source: CIA World Factbook 2008.

is first to dance with his daughter, followed by friends and relatives who request a dance. The party continues with different dances and kinds of music—modern, rock, country, or folkloric.

The coming-out party for boys is much simpler and takes place when they turn 18. Following a meal of *asado*, there is music and dancing. Then it's outside for a game of soccer.

Two views of Buenos Aires: the Casa Rosada (Pink House), Argentina's presidential mansion, facing the Plaza de Mayo (*opposite*); brightly painted houses in La Boca (*right*), a neighborhood settled in the 19th century by Italian immigrants.

5 Major Cities of Argentina

ARGENTINA IS HIGHLY urbanized. About 90 percent of the population lives in towns and cities. With 12.5 million inhabitants (2 million in the city proper), Buenos Aires and its suburbs form the largest metropolitan area in the country. Other large cities include Córdoba, Mendoza, Rosario, La Plata, and San Miguel de Tucumán.

Buenos Aires

Buenos Aires, meaning "good winds," lies on the South Atlantic coast along the Paraná River estuary known as the Río de la Plata. Its climate is generally pleasant with hot, humid summers, cool to cold winters, and comfortable spring and fall temperatures.

Spanish colonists established the permanent settlement of Buenos Aires in 1580. During the late 19th and early 20th centuries the city received millions of European immigrants, primarily Italians and Spaniards. The city also has a large Jewish community, as well as numerous descendants of English immigrants.

Today, Buenos Aires dominates Argentina in every way. More than one-third of the country's 37 million people live in the city and its suburbs. The city is the political, economic, social, and cultural center of Argentina. The nation's largest and finest universities are located there, too. Buenos Aires is also one of Argentina's major shipping, industrial, and commercial centers. Railroad lines converge from every corner of the nation, bringing goods for export, including meat, grain, motor vehicles, consumer goods, and textiles.

In Buenos Aires, the old and the new exist side by side. Historic European-style buildings and avenues mingle with modern high-rise apartment buildings, shopping malls, and department stores. Glass skyscrapers cast their slender shadows on 19th-century Victorian houses.

Buenos Aires has no major monument or urban square that serves as its focal point. Instead, the city is composed of many small neighborhoods. Each has its own character, colors, and forms. For instance, the San Telmo district, home to many artists, is noted for its mishmash of architectural styles. There are Spanish colonial houses with Italian detailing, along with graceful French classic buildings featuring antique shops, tango bars, and cafés.

Nineteenth-century Italian immigrant families painted La Boca's pressed tin houses a rainbow of colors. The houses, still bright today, are set off by colorful murals decorating the walls of side streets.

The city's most stylish neighborhood is the Barrio Recoleta. It's often

Córdoba, founded in 1573, remained Argentina's most important city until the rise of Buenos Aires in the late 19th century. Today visitors delight in Córdoba's charming colonial architecture. Shown here is the city's cathedral, which faces the Plaza San Martín.

called the Beverly Hills of Buenos Aires for its art galleries and upscale restaurants.

Buenos Aires boasts one of the world's finest opera houses. The Teatro Colón has hosted world-famous singers, dancers, and composers in its luxurious French Renaissance–style theater.

The Museo de Bellas Artes is Argentina's finest art museum. Folk art and modern Argentine painting are on display along with Impressionist and Postimpressionist paintings by Monet, Degas, and Chagall.

Any visitor to Buenos Aires should include a stop at the Plaza de Mayo. It's where citizens gathered to hear speeches by legendary *populist* leaders Juan and Evita Perón.

Visitors to Argentina's capital city are pleasantly surprised by the European energy buzzing in the South American air. The multiethnic residents reflect English, Italian, Spanish, or German heritage as well as South American roots. And, like European cities, Buenos Aires is known for its late-late-night dining and clubs. Buenos Aires is never more alive than at night.

Avenues fill with people on their way to restaurants and theaters. Residents of Argentina's capital enjoy dressing up and staying out. After dinner or a night of dancing, they like to grab a cup of coffee at one of the city's cafés and maybe watch the sunrise.

Córdoba

Córdoba, Argentina's old colonial capital, is a *picturesque* city of a million and a half people located on the edge of a mountain range known as the Sierra Chica. Before the rise of Buenos Aires, Córdoba was Argentina's center of arts and learning, a place of scholars and priests, churches and universities. Though in terms of national importance the city has fallen behind the capital, it retains a distinctive grace. Córdoba's name comes from the surrounding province, which embraces an unusually scenic section of the Andes, the Sierra de Córdoba.

The Primero River forms Córdoba's main natural landmark. The physical center is the Plaza San Martín, named for Argentina's great liberator and the site of the city's cathedral. South of the plaza is Calle Obispo Trejos, an avenue lined with some of the city's most illustrious colonial buildings, including the Compañía de Jesús Church, built in 1645.

Mar del Plata, located on the Atlantic coast south of Buenos Aires, is Argentina's most popular summer resort.

Argentina's 10 Largest Cities

#	City	Population	#	City	Population
1	**Buenos Aires** (metropolitan area)	12,955,300	6	**San Miguel de Tucumán**	796,900
2	**Córdoba**	1,460,500	7	**Mar del Plata**	668,600
3	**Rosario**	1,261,400	8	**Salta**	502,600
4	**Mendoza**	969,000	9	**Santa Fe**	502,200
5	**La Plata**	820,400	10	**San Juan**	439,000

Mar del Plata

If there is one place most Argentines like to go on their summer vacations, Mar del Plata is it. Located about 260 miles (418 km) south of Buenos Aires on the Atlantic Coast, Mar del Plata and its surrounding areas offer miles of some the best beaches in South America. Along with the natural beauty of the area's windswept dunes and dramatic cliffs, there are ecological reserves, fancy resorts, and charming fishing villages, plus the culture and vibrant nightlife of the city itself.

Compared with some of Argentina's other cities, Mar del Plata is young. It was founded in 1874 by a developer named Patricio Peralta Ramos, who turned the town into an industrial center. The true wealth of the city, though, came with the flood of tourism that took place during the last half of the 20th century. While many of the resorts were once reserved for the rich, today Mar del Plata is a favorite of middle-class families and students.

A Calendar of Argentine Festivals

Argentines celebrate a variety of local festivals, national civic holidays, and important Catholic feast days. Here are some of Argentina's best-known festivals and holidays.

JANUARY

In addition to celebrating **New Year's Day**, many Argentines take time out in January for the **National Festival of Folklore**. Held in Cosquín, in the central province of Córdoba, the festival also draws people from all over the world who are interested in folk traditions.

FEBRUARY

One of the largest celebrations throughout Argentina is **Carnaval** (which may be held in February or March, depending on when Easter falls in that particular year). Carnaval is celebrated just before Ash Wednesday, a traditional day of fasting that begins the Roman Catholic Lenten season about six weeks before Easter. In Argentina each region has its own Carnaval traditions. In the northern province of Salta, people dress up and dance the *zamba* and the *carnavalito*. In the northeastern provinces, people sing songs called *chamamé*, accompanied by accordions or harps.

MARCH

Two important festivals associated with food and drink take place in March. In the province of Mendoza, **La Fiesta de la Vendimia** is celebrated for three days during grape harvest season. Grapes are blessed on the vines, a queen is crowned, and wine-makers serve free red wine. The grand finale is an elaborate show of fireworks. This festival serves to remind people that their lives depend on the sun, rain, and earth.

At Mar del Plata on the coast, the **Harvest of Fish** is celebrated with a banquet of seafood and a parade of people dressed as sea creatures and led by the Queen of the Sea, riding in a seashell.

APRIL

More than 9 in 10 Argentines are Roman Catholic, and the Catholic Holy Week observances of **Holy Thursday, Good Friday, and Easter**—marking the Last Supper, Crucifixion, and Resurrection of Jesus Christ, respectively—are official holidays in Argentina. (Holy Week may fall in March.)

MAY

The 25th of the month is the anniversary of the **May Revolution**, a national holiday marking the date in 1810 when residents of Buenos Aires rose up against colonial authorities.

JUNE

Malvinas Day, June 10, is a national holiday that focuses attention on the islands Argentina has long claimed, and the British have long ruled under the name the Falklands.

Argentina's **Flag Day**, or Día de la Bandera, is June 20.

Argentines also celebrate a **Day of Friendship** every year at the end of June by send-

A Calendar of Argentine Festivals

ing out cards and calling their friends.

JULY

Argentina's **Independence Day**, celebrated July 9, commemorates the day in 1816 when leaders meeting in San Miguel de Tucumán proclaimed their complete independence from Spain and announced the formation of the United Provinces of South America (later to become the Republic of Argentina).

AUGUST

August 17 is a national holiday marking the **Death of General José de San Martín**, a leader in South America's struggle for independence from Spain. San Martín was born in a town along the Uruguay River in what is today Argentina.

Also in August, the southern Andean city of San Carlos de Bariloche hosts the popular **Snow Festival**. Many of the early settlers in this area came from Switzerland, and Swiss cake and hot port wine with cinnamon are served during the festival.

OCTOBER

October 12, **Columbus Day**, is a national holiday in Argentina.

DECEMBER

December features two religious holidays, the **Immaculate Conception** (December 8) and **Christmas**.

Argentines celebrate **New Year's Eve** with fireworks. The streets are filled with music and dancing, and in Buenos Aires there is a ticker-tape parade.

Musicians pound out the beat during a street parade in Buenos Aires.

Recipes

Locro (Argentine Vegetable Stew)

(Serves 4–5)
1/2 cup dried navy beans, soaked
1/4 cup whole wheat
1/4 cup barley
4 cups water
1 large piece calabaza squash, or 1 small butternut squash (about 1 pound)
1/2 lb boiling potatoes
1 large carrot
1 small sweet potato
1 cup frozen corn
2 bay leaves
1/2 tsp sea salt
2 whole scallions, chopped

Directions:
1. Drain the beans.
2. In a 4-quart pot, combine beans with barley, and add 3 cups of the water. Bring to a boil, reduce heat, and simmer covered, 15–20 minutes.
3. Meanwhile, cut squash, potatoes, carrots, and sweet potatoes into medium-sized chunks.
4. Add all vegetables, including corn and scallions, to the pot. Add remaining 1 cup water, bay leaves, and salt. Bring to a simmer.
5. Cook for 1 hour covered, over low heat. Stir occasionally. Vegetables should be soft; squash will disintegrate. To thicken stew, if needed, dissolve wheat flour into 1/4 cup of water and add to pot.

Argentine Potato Salad

(Serves 8)
1 large carrot, cut into 1/2" dice
6 white potatoes, peeled and cut into 1/2" dice
1 tbsp Dijon-style mustard
1 cup mayonnaise
2 tbsp sherry or red wine vinegar
2 tbsp finely minced onion
2 hard-boiled eggs, sliced
1/2 cup chopped parsley
1 cup sliced hearts of palm
1/2 cup sliced stuffed green olives
1 cup cooked (fresh or frozen) green peas
1 roasted red bell pepper cut in thin strips, or pimento pieces
1 green apple such as Granny Smith, cut into 1/2" dice (optional)

Directions:
1. Cook carrot in boiling water, covered, until medium tender, about 15 minutes. Drain and cool.
2. Boil potatoes in water. Cover until medium tender, 8 to 10 minutes. Drain and cool.
3. Combine mustard, mayonnaise, sherry, and onion.
4. Put potatoes, carrot, apple, peas, and eggs in large bowl. Carefully fold in mayonnaise sauce.
5. Season to taste with salt and pepper.
6. Put salad on oval platter and garnish with parsley, hearts of palm, olives, and roasted red pepper.

Mushroom Tortilla

(Serves 8)
6 big Portobello mushrooms
1 half-inch-wide bacon slice, cut in small squares
5 well-beaten eggs
Salt and pepper

Directions:

1. Wash the mushrooms. Cut them into small pieces.
2. Fry the bacon, adding the mushrooms when there is grease.
3. Pour in the beaten eggs. Scramble.
4. Spoon mixture into warm flour tortillas.
Goes well with a salad.

Dulce de Leche

(Serves 3–4)
1 quart milk
1 cup sugar
1 tsp vanilla
6 slices of white bread, shredded
2 egg yolks, beaten
Cinnamon to taste

Directions:

1. Cook the milk together with the sugar, vanilla, and cinnamon, stirring constantly.
2. When milk begins to thicken, add bread (very finely shredded) and continue stirring.
3. When mixture gets very thick, remove from heat and beat thoroughly. While it is still warm, add the well-beaten egg yolks and let the batch cool.
4. Refrigerate until ready to use.

Sandy Lemon Cookies

(Makes about 3 dozen cookies)
1 cup margarine
1 cup sugar
3 egg yolks
1 tbsp brandy
1 tsp vanilla
Grated zest of 1/2 lemon
2 1/4 cup cornstarch
1 3/4 cup flour
1/2 tsp baking soda
2 tsp baking powder

Filling: *dulce de leche* and grated coconut

Directions:

1. Preheat oven to 350°.
2. Beat the margarine with sugar; add egg yolks one by one and beat well. Add brandy, vanilla, and grated lemon zest.
3. In a separate bowl, mix cornstarch, flour, baking soda, and baking powder. Slowly stir in liquid from step #2 to make a soft dough.
4. Roll out about 1/4 inch thick and cut out with a 2-inch cookie cutter.
5. Bake on greased cookie sheets approximately 12 minutes (the cookies don't change color).
6. Remove very carefully from cookie sheets with a metal spatula. When cool, butter insides of two cookies with cold *dulce de leche*. Add a sprinkle of grated coconut. Press together.

Glossary

alluvial—composed of material (such as clay, silt, sand, and gravel) deposited by flowing water.

compulsory—required, usually by law.

continental divide—an extensive stretch of high ground from each side of which the river systems of a continent flow in opposite directions.

cordillera—a long chain of mountains or mountain ranges.

coup—a sudden takeover of a government by force, usually by a small group.

devaluation—an official reduction in the exchange value of a currency.

estuary—the arm of the sea that goes inland to meet the mouth of a river.

Fascist—a member of a political party, or characteristic of a political movement, that emerged in the mid-20th century and that elevated the state above the individual, supported dictatorial rule, and advocated social regimentation.

flax—a plant that yields fine textile fiber and linseed oil.

frontier—the area along an international border.

gross domestic product (GDP)—the total value of goods and services produced by a country over a year's time.

indigenous—native to an area.

inflation—the increasing cost of goods and services in an economy over a period of time.

junta—a group of military officers ruling a country.

literacy—the ability to read and write.

nomadic—moving about; wandering.

picturesque—charming in appearance; suitable for a picture.

populist—a member of a political party claiming to support the rights and power of the common people over those of vested interests.

protectionism—a policy that favors a country's business interests against foreign competition.

savanna—flat grassland of tropical or subtropical regions.

Project and Report Ideas

Exploded Map

Make a map of Argentina's six distinct regions. Then cut the six pieces apart and glue them to a posterboard. Beside each, add a one-paragraph description of the region.

Argentine Wild Animal Park

Imagine a wild animal park that provides a home for animals native to Argentina. Design your wild animal park, showing where species are located. Add a two-sentence description for each type of animal. For ideas, see the interactive map of the San Diego Wild Animal Park at **http://www.sandiegozoo.org/wap/wap_map.html.**

Comparison Bar Graph

Create a bar graph showing the populations of the 10 largest cities in Argentina and the 10 largest in the United States. Use two colors.

Biographies

Write a one-page biography of one the following figures from Argentina's history:

- Juan de Solís
- Sebastian Cabot
- Roberto M. Ortiz
- Jorge Luis Borges
- Juan D. Perón
- Evita Perón

History Reports

Write one-page reports explaining these events in Argentina's history:

- The founding of Buenos Aires
- The rise of the gauchos
- The creation of the tango
- The Dirty War
- The Falkland Islands War

Project and Report Ideas

Resources Map

Make a map showing where Argentina's resources are located (many encyclopedias show this information).

Project for Two Students: Travel Bureau

Go to Virtual Tourist.com. Visit the page
    www.virtualtourist.com/m/.157962/1639/?s=I
at which a young American describes her travel experiences in Buenos Aires. Write a script about someone coming into a travel agency who has to take a business trip to Buenos Aires. The travel agent should describe things to see and do, based on the advice at the website. Also, include in your script travel costs such as airfare, lodging, and meals.

Project for Two Students: "Doubling the Cape"

In his famous book *Two Years Before the Mast*, about his teenage years sailing out of San Diego in the 1830s, Richard Henry Dana describes in vivid detail the treacherous trip around the tip of South America. At that time, going near the bottom of the world was the only way to reach the Atlantic Ocean traveling east from the Pacific. From Dana's book, read the chapter "Doubling the Cape." Using a map, show classmates the route and summarize the dangers that sailors faced in that part of the world. Choose an especially good passage from the book and read it aloud. Make sure you rehearse it.

Chronology

1516	Juan de Solís, the first Spanish explorer to reach the region, is killed by native people.
1526	Sebastian Cabot sails up the Paraná and Paraguay Rivers; he stays for four years and calls the area "Argentina," meaning "of silver."
1620	The Spanish viceroyalty of Peru assumes control of the Río de la Plata region.
1776	The huge territory occupied by present-day Argentina, Bolivia, Paraguay, and Uruguay is separated from Peru and incorporated as the Viceroyalty of the Río de la Plata.
1810	Colonial patriots in Buenos Aires oust the Spanish viceregal government.
1816	On July 9, colonists proclaim their complete independence from Spain and announce the formation of the United Provinces of South America.
1819	A brief civil war breaks out; the next decade is plagued by political chaos in the absence of a strong central government.
1829	General Juan Manuel de Rosas is elected president of the Buenos Aires Province; he gradually brings other provinces under his dictatorial control in the Argentine Confederation.
1852	Rosas is ousted.
1853	A federal constitution, similar in language and content to the United States Constitution, is adopted; the Argentine Republic is established.
1862	After two wars between the Buenos Aires Province and the other provinces of the Argentine Republic, a national convention elects General Bartolomé Mitre to the presidency and designates the city of Buenos Aires as the national capital.
1943	A group of military officers seizes control of the government; General Pedro Ramírez assumes the presidency and outlaws political parties.
1944	A military junta under the leadership of Colonel Juan D. Perón seizes power.
1946	Perón is elected to the presidency; his popular wife, Evita, is put in charge of labor and health relations.
1951	Perón is reelected president with a huge majority.
1952	Evita Perón dies of cancer; Juan Perón's support begins to decline.

Chronology

1955	In September, after three days of bloody fighting, a military coup succeeds in ousting Perón, who goes into exile; the federal constitution of 1853 is restored.
1973	In June, after Argentina is wracked by a period of terrorist violence, Perón returns to Buenos Aires; he becomes president in September.
1974	Perón dies in July, succeeded by third wife Isabel; escalating terrorism leaves hundreds dead.
1976	A military junta under General Jorge Videla seizes power; opponents of the regime are rounded up in the so-called Dirty War, during which thousands of people are murdered.
1981	General Leopoldo Galtieri heads the military regime.
1982	Argentine soldiers occupy the British-held Falkland Islands; more than 700 Argentines are killed in the Falklands War, which British forces win; Galtieri resigns.
1983	Argentina returns to civilian rule; inflation runs at more than 900 percent.
1989	Carlos Saúl Menem is elected president; he institutes economic reforms that emphasize the selling of state-owned enterprises to private interests.
1992	Argentina introduces a new currency, the peso, which is pegged to the U.S. dollar.
1999	Fernando de la Rua wins the presidency, inheriting a $114 billion public debt.
2000	The International Monetary Fund grants Argentina an aid package of nearly $40 billion.
2001	Public workers go on a 24-hour, nationwide strike to protest new governmental curbs on bank withdrawals and a delay in pension payouts.
2002	Congress selects Peronist senator Eduardo Duhalde to finish de la Rua's term; days later, the government devalues the peso; ongoing riots and demonstrations signal anger with Argentina's economic situation.
2003	Peronist Néstor Kirchner is elected president; Supreme Court overturns court immunity of former military officers suspected of Dirty War atrocities.
2007	Cristina Fernández de Kirchner, former senator and first lady, is elected president.
2010	Argentina's government attempts to prevent British companies from drilling for oil in the Atlantic waters off the Faulkland Islands.

Further Reading/Internet Resources

Adams, Fiona. *Argentina: A Survival Guide to Customs and Etiquette.* Tarrytown, N.Y.: Marshall Cavendish, 2007.

Blashfield, Jean F. *Argentina.* New York: Children's Press, 2007.

Palmerlee, Danny. *Argentina.* Oakland, Calif.: Lonely Planet, 2008.

Stille, Darlene R. *Eva Perón: First Lady of Argentina.* Mankato, Minn.: Compass Point Books, 2006.

Streissguth, Thomas. *Argentina in Pictures.* Minneapolis: Lerner Publications, 2003.

History and Geography

http://www.geographia.com/argentina/argen01.htm
http://www.unep-wcmc.org/forest/data/country/arg.htm
http://travel.state.gov/travel/cis_pa_tw/cis/cis_1130.html
http://www.geographia.com/argentina/index.html

Economic and Political Information

https://www.cia.gov/library/publications/the-world-factbook/geos/ar.html
http://www.economist.com/Countries/Argentina/

Culture and Festivals

http://www.lonelyplanet.com/worldguide/argentina/
http://www.iexplore.com/dmap/Argentina/Culture
http://www.surdelsur.com/pagina3ingles.html

For More Information

The Argentine Embassy
1600 New Hampshire Ave., NW
Washington, DC 20009
(202) 238-6400
http://athea.ar/cwash/homepage

Argentina Government Tourist Office
12 West 56th St.
New York, NY 10019
(212) 603-0443
http://www.wam.com.ar/tourism/

Embassy of the United States of America
Avenida Colombia 4300
C1425GMN Buenos Aires
Argentina
http://usembassy.state.gov/posts/ar1/wwwh0100.html

Index

Index/Picture Credits

Contributors

Senior Consulting Editor **James D. Henderson** is professor of international studies at Coastal Carolina University. He is the author of *Conservative Thought in Twentieth Century Latin America: The Ideals of Laureano Gómez* (1988; Spanish edition *Las ideas de Laureano Gómez* published in 1985); *When Colombia Bled: A History of the Violence in Tolima* (1985; Spanish edition *Cuando Colombia se desangró, una historia de la Violencia en metrópoli y provincia*, 1984); and co-author of *A Reference Guide to Latin American History* (2000) and *Ten Notable Women of Latin America* (1978).

Mr. Henderson earned a bachelor's degree in history from Centenary College of Louisiana, and a master's degree in history from the University of Arizona. He then spent three years in the Peace Corps, serving in Colombia, before earning his doctorate in Latin American history in 1972 at Texas Christian University.

Charles J. Shields is the author of 20 books for young people. He has degrees in English and history from the University of Illinois, Urbana-Champaign. Before turning to writing full time, he was chairman of the English and guidance departments at Homewood-Flossmoor High School in Flossmoor, Illinois. He lives in Homewood, a suburb of Chicago, with his wife, Guadalupe, a former elementary school principal and now an educational consultant to the Chicago Public Schools.